Science
Foundation Plus
Activity Book A

Published by Collins
An imprint of HarperCollins*Publishers*
The News Building, 1 London Bridge Street,
London, SE1 9GF, UK

HarperCollins*Publishers*
Macken House, 39/40 Mayor Street Upper,
Dublin 1, D01 C9W8, Ireland

Browse the complete Collins catalogue at
www.collins.co.uk

ISBN 978-0-00-846873-6

British Library Cataloguing-in-Publication Data
A catalogue record for this publication is available from the British Library.

Author: Fiona Macgregor
Publisher: Elaine Higgleton
Product manager: Letitia Luff
Commissioning editor: Rachel Houghton
Researcher: Andi Colombo
Edited by: Eleanor Barber
Editorial management: Oriel Square
Cover designer: Kevin Robbins
Cover illustrations: Jouve India Pvt Ltd.
Internal illustrations: Jouve India Pvt. Ltd; p 7 Tasneem Amiruddin, p 22 Stu Mclellan
Typesetter: Jouve India Pvt. Ltd.
Production controller: Lyndsey Rogers
Printed and bound in India by
Replika Press Pvt. Ltd.

Acknowledgements

With thanks to all the kindergarten staff and their schools around the world who have helped with the development of this course, by sharing insights and commenting on and testing sample materials:

Calcutta International School: Sharmila Majumdar, Mrs Pratima Nayar, Preeti Roychoudhury, Tinku Yadav, Lakshmi Khanna, Mousumi Guha, Radhika Dhanuka, Archana Tiwari, Urmita Das; Gateway College (Sri Lanka): Kousala Benedict; Hawar International School: Kareen Barakat, Shahla Mohammed, Jennah Hussain; Manthan International School: Shalini Reddy; Monterey Pre-Primary: Adina Oram; Prometheus School: Aneesha Sahni, Deepa Nanda; Pragyanam School: Monika Sachdev; Rosary Sisters High School: Samar Sabat, Sireen Freij, Hiba Mousa; Solitaire Global School: Devi Nimmagadda; United Charter Schools (UCS): Tabassum Murtaza; Vietnam Australia International School: Holly Simpson

The publishers wish to thank the following for permission to reproduce photographs.

(t = top, c = centre, b = bottom, r = right, l = left)

p 4tl Alice Reece/Getty Images, p 4tr Ye Choh Wah/Shutterstock, p 4cl Rolf Nussbaumer Photography/Alamy Stock Photo, p 4cr Minden Pictures/Richard Du Toit/Getty Images, p 4bl Minden Pictures/Ch'ien Lee/Getty Images, p 4br Minden Pictures/Donald M Jones/Getty Images, p 6 kdshutterman/Shutterstock, p 9tl JHK2303/Shutterstock, p 9tc M. Unal Ozmen/Shutterstock, p 9tr amenic181/Shutterstock, p 9cl Studioimagen73/Shutterstock, p 9c Vector things/Shutterstock, p 9cr Mega Pixel/Shutterstock, p 9cl2 Alexlukin/Shutterstock, p 9bl BW Folsom/Shutterstock, p 9bc Pixfiction/Shutterstock, p 9br Tim UR/Shutterstock, p 16t1 Ilona Ignatova/Shutterstock, p 16t2 Kletr/Shutterstock, p 16c Mircea BEZERGHEANU/Shutterstock, p 16b1 artjazz/Shutterstock, p 16b2 worldswildlifewonders/Shutterstock, p 22b1 Tom Wang/Shutterstock, p 22b2 Wanwalee Wong/Shutterstock

MIX
Paper | Supporting responsible forestry
FSC™ C007454

Find

   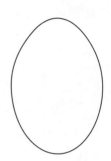

  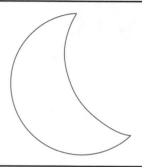 

Find the things that are the same.
Colour them in using the same colour.   Date:

Find and circle

   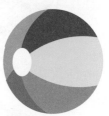

Find and circle the biggest thing in each row.

Date:

Find

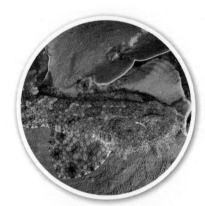

Find the animals in the pictures.
Can you name some of them?

Date:

How many?

<table>
<tr><td></td><td></td><td></td></tr>
<tr><td></td><td></td><td></td></tr>
<tr><td></td><td></td><td></td></tr>
<tr><td></td><td></td><td></td></tr>
</table>

---------------   ---------------   ---------------

PCM 2. Draw the counters on your table.
Count them and write the number.   Date:

Match

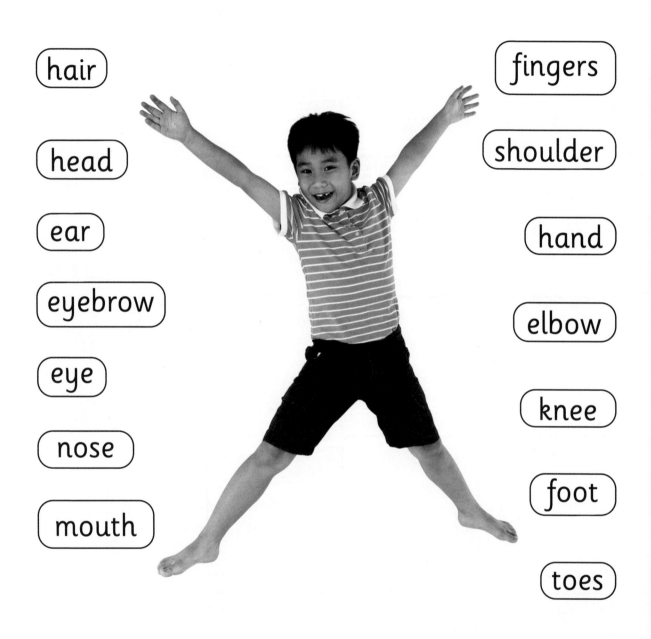

hair

head

ear

eyebrow

eye

nose

mouth

fingers

shoulder

hand

elbow

knee

foot

toes

Match the labels to the parts of the body.

Date:

Count and colour

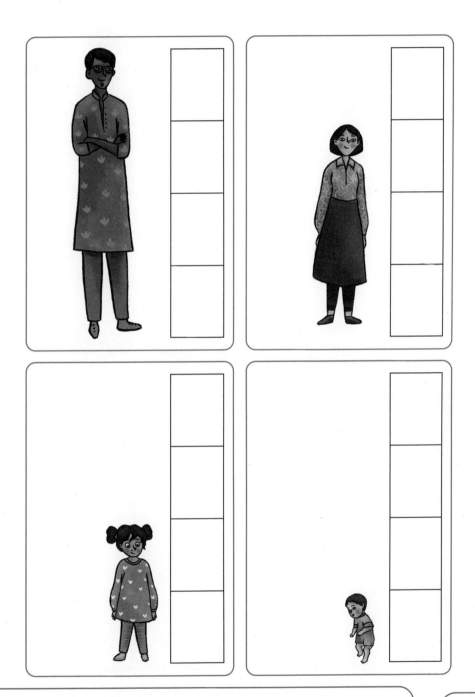

Colour the boxes to show how tall each person is.

Draw a ● next to the tallest person.

Draw a ▇ next to the shortest person.

Date:

Sort

Healthy foods	Unhealthy foods

PCM 3. Stick the healthy foods in the green box.
Stick the unhealthy foods in the blue box.

Date:

Circle

Choose a healthy meal.

Date:

Cut and stick

I [　　　　　　　　] with my 👃 .

I [　　　　　　　　] with my 👁 .

I [　　　　　　　　] with my 👂 .

I [　　　　　　　　] with my 👄 .

I [　　　　　　　　] with my ✋ .

PCM 4. Cut out the labels. Stick them in the
correct place. Read the sentences.   Date:

Colour

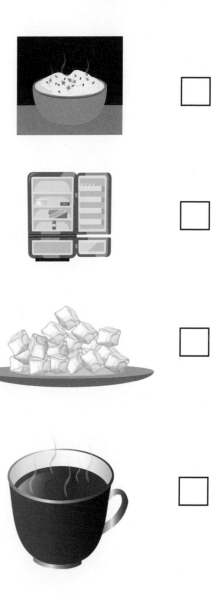

Colour the box red for things that are hot.
Colour the box blue for things that are cold.   Date:

Draw

Draw your favourite food.

Date:

Circle

1

2

1 Circle the things you can smell.
2 Circle the things you can hear.

Date:

Count and colour

Count the animals. Colour in 1 block for each animal.

Date:

Find and colour

legs	wings	horns	hooves
tail	head	paws	ears
	body	eyes	

Colour the words that match the parts of the goat.
Colour in the goat.

Date:

Match and say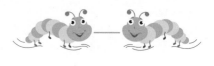

Has slimy skin

It is an **amphibian.**

Has hair or fur

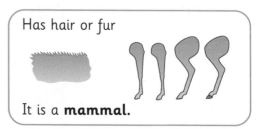

It is a **mammal.**

Lives in water

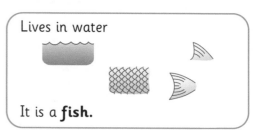

It is a **fish.**

Has feathers

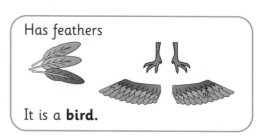

It is a **bird.**

Has six legs

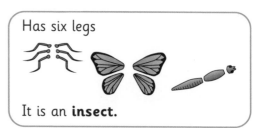

It is an **insect.**

Match the animals to the words and pictures.

Date:

Circle

Circle the animal that is different in each row.

Date:

Find and colour

Find the seeds that are the same. Colour them in
using the same colour.   Date:

Say and colour

Colour the flower yellow; colour the stem green; colour the leaves green;
colour the roots brown; colour the soil brown.   Date:

Put in order

1	2
3	4

PCM 8. Cut out the pictures and stick them in the correct order.

Date:

Draw

My plant is _____ days old.

Draw the plant you are growing.
How old is your plant?   Date:

Revie

Match

We are living things.

Which animals are the same?

I use my senses.

Plants are living things too.

Match the sentences to the pictures.

Date:

Tick

☐ I can find.

☐ I can count.

☐ I can match.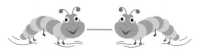

☐ I can sort.

☐ I can circle.

☐ I can cut and stick.

☐ I can find and colour.

☐ I can draw.

☐ I can look and say.

Tick what you can do.

Date:

Assessment record

_____ has achieved these Science Foundation Plus Phase Objectives:

Using one criterion, compare things, finding similarities and differences	1	2	3
Take measurements using a range of informal units	1	2	3
Record observations and measurements by completing simple tables	1	2	3
Identify and name the main external parts of the human body	1	2	3
Recognise that humans are all similar in some ways but that every person is unique	1	2	3
Recognise that we can behave in ways that help us to stay fit and healthy	1	2	3
Identify healthy foods	1	2	3
Carry out some observation tasks	1	2	3
Investigate sounds and experiment with loud and soft sounds	1	2	3
Identify different tastes and favourite foods	1	2	3
Identify different smells	1	2	3
Discuss touch and texture	1	2	3
Recognise different animal parts	1	2	3
Identify basic external parts of common animals and use these to group animals	1	2	3
Classify seeds using observable properties	1	2	3
Recognise that living things change as they grow	1	2	3
Reognise the difference between rock and soil/sand	1	2	3
Observe, measure and record data in a plant diary	1	2	3

1: Partially achieved
2: Achieved
3: Exceeded

Signed by teacher:
Signed by parent: Date: